A BOOK OF VALUES

Your Personal Guide to Meaning and Happiness

ALAN KOVITZ

A BOOK OF VALUES

Your Personal Guide to Meaning and Happiness

Copyright © Alan Kovitz

Disclaimer

This book contains the ideas and opinions of its author. The intention of this book is to provide information, helpful content, and motivation to readers about the subjects addressed. It is published and sold with the understanding that the author is not engaged to render any type of psychological, medical, legal, or any other kind of personal or professional advice. No warranties or guarantees are expressed or implied by the author's choice to include any of the content in this volume. The author shall not be liable for any physical, psychological, emotional, financial, or commercial damages, including, but not limited to, special, incidental, consequential, or other damages. The reader is responsible for their own choices, actions, and results.

1st Edition. 1st printing 2021

Cover Design & Interior Design: Steve Walters, Oxygen Publishing Inc.

Editor: Richard Tardif

Independently Published by
Oxygen Publishing Inc.
Montreal, QC, Canada
www.oxygenpublishing.com

ISBN: 978-1-990093-32-6

Imprint: Independently published

52 Values

1. Relationships
2. Vision
3. Passion
4. Joy
5. Balance
6. Grit
7. Humor
8. Trust
9. Gratitude
10. Forgiveness
11. Frivolity
12. Vacation
13. Continuity
14. Spirit
15. Faith
16. Friendship
17. Truth
18. Honesty
19. Charity
20. Action
21. Rest
22. Intensity
23. Fairness
24. Love
25. Duty
26. Honor
27. Invincibility
28. Cunning
29. Heart
30. Pride
31. Self
32. Camaraderie
33. Simplicity
34. Competition
35. Celebration
36. Inspiration
37. Creativity
38. Imagination
39. Communication
40. Presence
41. Resourcefulness
42. Renewal
43. Courage
44. Curiosity
45. Focus
46. Family
47. Wellness
48. Authenticity
49. Adventure
50. Connection
51. Kindness
52. Inclusion

Dedication

This book would never have been completed without the gracious assistance of my friend, colleague, and writing coach Tracy Lunquist. When inspiration lacked, or words were difficult to find, she was there. Her belief in me, and this project, continually prodded the very best out of myself. I am forever in her debt.

I would also recognize my family for their wonderful support. My partner Angie, our children and grandchildren, are the base from which ideas germinate. I love and cherish them all.

Several in the family offered to read the manuscript of this book in its infancy, offering ideas and encouragement. Their insistence on reading the words drove me further down the path. Angela Lewis, Rebekah Lee, Rhiannon Williams, and Brandon Kovitz - I am grateful.

Preface

The idea for a book of values emerged over time as a facilitator and business coach. Values, I discovered, bridges the gap between current and desired performance, unlocking the hidden potential for happiness in our personal lives, and invariably, in our business lives. The pursuit of happiness became my obsession. My purpose in writing this book is to guide you in your pursuit of happiness, to stand beside you, to mentor you, to support you in your pursuit.

The 52 values described in this book contribute to human wholeness. I believe every one of them is important. I also recognize that some of them seem like they oppose each other. That is intentional too. People are wonderfully complicated! And to be whole means to embrace it, struggle with it, grow into and through it.

It's also worth noting that while every value is a good thing to build into your life, it's not possible or practical to live all of them fully all the time. One way you can use this book is to help figure out your Core Values. Core Values are the half-dozen (give or take a few) values that you prioritize over others. If something has to give, then it is clearly something other than your Core Values. Like the Boar's Head deli ads say: "Compromise elsewhere."

As you read each value and its description, think about how important that value is to you. Which values stand out as the guiding principles you live by? If you look at a pair of values that seem to oppose each other, which one feels more like you?

You can read the 52 values in any order, as much or as little as you desire. I'd read one passage per week for a year and spend time with it. Read the same passage every day for a week. Keep the book with you, so you can re-read or take notes whenever something comes to mind. Talk about it with family and friends. Decide what you agree with and where you think I'm full of baloney. Maybe even write your paragraph or page about what you think the value word means, and why it's important — or why it's not!

Each value comes with a Mantra, and a Question. The Mantra is an example of an affirmation for that Value, something you could use to reinforce your belief or practice of that value. The Question is an invitation to explore the value more deeply, considering its ins and outs, and its impact on you and those you care about.

See what happens when you engage with the ideas I've offered? At the end of one year, see if you feel more whole.

Where This Idea Started

In my 35-plus-years career of coaching, I've had the pleasure of working with thousands of leaders of small to midsize organizations. We spent much of that time creating strategic plans — the roadmaps that great organizations traveled to get to where they want to go. One component of great strategic plans is the formulation of the organization's Core Values - the three to seven guideposts of behavior that direct all participants in how to do their "jobs." These are the non-negotiable values that drive every aspect of the "how" of the organization's work — and, by extension, form the heart of its culture. Anyone deviating from the chosen Core Values either doesn't understand them or disagrees with them. Those that cannot follow the organization's chosen culture, as outlined in the Core Values, will either change or leave.

The creation of Core Values is difficult. I've found plenty of leaders unable to tackle this onerous task. It is difficult to define the specific culture that will correctly propel the organization toward its vision. Many simply ignore this step or do a poor job of defining the correct Core Values, derailing success. I've seen the frustration on leaders' faces as they meander without values.

That leads to this; to elegantly create your organization's culture through the definition of Core Values, you must have your personal values squared away, and most leaders have yet to define those values.

It is this observation that led me to shift the focus of my practice, from organizational work to individual coaching of leaders. And those experiences led me to write this book to offer you the chance to explore your values. When you determine which values fit you the best, they will feel so right that you will live by them every day as you march toward fulfilling your vision.

Thanks for picking up this book. Enjoy the journey!

Love,

Alan

Introduction

What are Values?

Values are the non-negotiable principles that guide the way we each show up in the world. They ride alongside our attitudes and beliefs, and drive our choices and behaviors. When we are living our values, it feels right. If living our values means making a sacrifice, losing something we care about, or making an unpopular choice, it may not feel good, but it feels right.

Sometimes we make a choice that goes against our values because that choice feels good in the moment, or is expedient, but it rarely works out in the long run. In fact, sometimes those unpleasant experiences are how we discover our Core Values — coming to realize after the fact that the choice we made was out of sync with who we truly want to be. Another definition of values might be, "values are the traits in ourselves that we want to cultivate."

Most people haven't taken the time and thoughtful effort to figure out their Core Values. That you picked up this book means you are not "most people"! For whatever reason, something made you curious enough about values to open this book and read this page. My invitation to you is to do the worthwhile work of discovering your Core Values.

Spend a full week with each value. Besides reading the passage each day for a week and engaging with it in conversations with family and friends, you could also do some writing or journaling. For example, you could write a story of a time when you lived this value, or a time when you didn't, and how that worked out. Ask yourself the question, "if this were one of my Core Values, what would that look like?" and write out some examples of behaviors that reflect that value.

Part of what will happen in this process is that you'll decide what your Core Values aren't. It isn't practical to focus on 52 different (and sometimes conflicting) values all the time, but you may come to understand that at least 40 of the values in this book are not critically important to you on a day-to-day basis. And that's great! The surest path to emotional burnout is to be all things to all people. You serve the world best by being the unique individual you are. When you focus on your strengths, they become even stronger!

Ultimately, words are just words. It is your behavior — how you speak, how you act, and how you interact with others — that shows the world your true values. As you explore different values, think about how much genuine effort and action you are taking to support that value, and what you want to do differently.

1

Relationships

We live in a global society. Our ability to survive and thrive depends on our desire and capability to create and sustain lasting human relationships. On the simplest level, we interact to survive and reproduce. To thrive, we need deep and meaningful connections with other human beings.

Relationships are important both personally and professionally.

On the personal side, we are born into a family of at least a single parent. Often, a family includes two parents and perhaps brothers and sisters, or other relatives living under the same roof. The bonds formed early in childhood between us and our families shape us as adults. Healthy parenting provides safety, stability, and a road map to guide children as they grow into adulthood and become parents. Unhealthy Relationships early in childhood create enormous, but not insurmountable, obstacles as adults. Loving parents and families shape loving children who enrich the world with compassion, energy, and spirit.

Professionally, success is grounded in relationships. Building a business depends on creating mutually beneficial relationships. Sales success lies in building a base of loyal customers, and customers become loyal because of these relationships. Sustainable commerce depends on creating lasting bonds built on trust. Our business relationships should be ones of mutual gain, with no one party exploiting an advantage to hold over others.

When Relationships are one of your core values, you might also prize trust, communication, and friendship, or all of these. You devote considerable time and energy to nurturing your relationships. You might attempt to find synergies among people you know, helping to connect people who may benefit from knowing one another. In a difficult situation, you may compromise on other things that matter to you in order to maintain trust and harmony.

Mantra:

My relationships are essential
to my happiness and success.

Question: Are all of my relationships feeding my happiness and success? If not, what needs to change?

2

Vision

Consider Vision the synopsis of everything you desired for the future — what it looks, feels and seems like in all its glory and extravagance. It is ours to draw up as a pop-up picture book, complete with details not found in standard business plans. Where we will be, what we will do, and with whom — are contained in the pages of this book. What perfect colors will you surround yourself with? Who do you wish to become? You, and only you, are the creator of your amazing future.

Without a compelling vision, a person may meander aimlessly through life, taking things as they come. Wandering back and forth with no map, compass, or a planned destination makes us reactive to everything we find on the road. We make dramatic course changes with no confidence that we have found a better path. We stumble on unforeseen potholes large enough to swallow our souls. We might decide to create a Bucket List, a ledger of things for us to accomplish before we die, but often we don't start making the list until middle age. Shouldn't we work on this earlier in our lives? What if we instead created a Dream List, or Dream Inventory, starting from the moment we learn to write? We can inspire our children to make dreaming and vision part of their normal, everyday thinking. What are we waiting for?

When you have a clear vision as a core value, you easily and elegantly avoid many of life's potholes, because you have devoted significant effort to building a detailed picture of the life you desire, and you connect frequently to that picture. Events often seem to fall in your favor, propelling you toward your desires and fulfilling your listed dreams. Things fall into place naturally, as if the world exists just for you. Those things you most want and need appear as if summoned magically by wand. It's not an effortless process, but because of your singleness of purpose and clarity of vision, things go your way more often than not.

Mantra:

I see my desired future in high definition.

Question: In what areas of my life do I need to invest more time in visioning, to see things more clearly?

3
Passion

Imagine living every day with no drive or determination to accomplish what needs to be accomplished. Getting up in the morning, dreading the drive to the office or amble down the hall to your home office. You feel like what you're doing makes little sense, as if the world has turned upside down and is throwing you off. Imagine further, walking through life as a zombie (and haven't you had enough of that?) lacking any zest, other than to get through another day. Fretting every minute of every day...

This happens to people with no passion for what they do — or for life. When you embrace your life with passion, you do what you love and love what you do every minute of every day. There is no drudgery here, only a powerful calling to make a difference using the strengths that have surfaced, as you relentlessly pursue personal growth and understanding.

How do you find your passion? There can be many ways: the "feeling-out" process of trying divergent ventures, being employed in various fields, opening a new door whenever one closes, recognizing when you are in a state of bliss, or gratitude, or "flow." Notice that these involve actions and trying different ways without fear of failure. We know we learn more from failure than success, and passionate people know they may experience many failures on the path to ultimate victory.

When passion is one of your core values, you embrace it every day as a gift. You bring your full life force to everything you do, and if faced with the choice to do something by half-measure, you simply don't do it at all. You may find yourself drawn to others who also have great passion. Your loved ones, if they understand you, will clear a path for you to engage them and everything else through your passion — the ultimate feeling of desire.

Mantra:

Damn the torpedoes! Full speed ahead!

Question: In what areas of my life (if any) am I not feeling passion? What can I change?

4
Joy

I f you ever saw the Pixar movie Inside Out, the first character you met was Joy, presented as the first and only emotion that exists in a newborn baby. For a good portion of the movie, she also does everything in her power to keep her human host happy, reasoning that Joy is the best possible emotional state at all times.

As a value, Joy is about reveling in environments, and experiences as they happen. It goes deeper than happiness, as the Joy character in the movie learns throughout the story, capturing not just those times when we feel cheerful, but when we feel deeply content and grateful for the present moment. Life without Joy is grim and grey. Those who struggle with chronic depression or other emotional disorders can speak to how difficult it is just to get out of bed in the morning, when Joy remains out of reach for long stretches of time. And it's a bit of a double-edged sword. If we never had rough times in our lives, never felt sad, lonely, angry, or discontent, we might not recognize or savor the gift of Joy when it comes.

If you have Joy as a core value, you understand the difference between true Joy and happiness. You do not expect to be happy all the time, and you do not seek to sugar-coat your life or the world. Instead, you are attentive to the good things that happen around you. You pay attention to sensations, like a warm breeze on your face or the feel of ice cream melting on your tongue, or the moments of connection with other people. You love to laugh and to do or say things that bring happiness to others. When you are experiencing Joy, you are aware of how it feels and what has brought it about, and you devote time and energy to creating and recreating those moments.

Mantra:

I savor the moments of joy in my life.

Question: What are my greatest sources of joy? How can I reflect my joy back to its source and extend it to others?

5
Balance

A key milestone on the journey to wholeness is finding balance. On the surface, Balance might seem simple, like yin and yang: you achieve it by somehow placing equal emphasis or devoting equal effort to the key aspects of your life like the popular, or should we say, overused idea of "work-life balance". We know people who are so driven to succeed at their careers that they give short shrift to their home lives, staying late at the office and missing little Johnny's ball game. It's almost a cliché, and certainly one to avoid. True Balance is so much more than that! It's about creating and pursuing a colorful array of goals and actions that together comprise the palette of your life. Making a living is important, yes. But making a life is about discovering the most meaningful, most fulfilling experiences from the universe of choices available to you. Time for exercise, quality time with your partner, family or friends, alone time, playtime with kids (yours or someone else's), service to a community or cause that matters to you—hobbies, travel, and even walking the dog can be part of building a complete and satisfying life.

Too many people focus on whatever is right in front of them at a moment, that they never stop to consider what they hope to achieve, or even to experience in their lifetimes. Lacking vision, they live in a reactive way, and inevitably end up out of balance. If you want to become whole, you must know what wholeness looks like for you. That includes understanding how much of your energy you wish to devote to each of the parts of that whole.

When Balance is one of your core values, you recognize the importance of taking the long view, and of being intentional about how you invest your time and energy. You understand that balance is a long-term, not a short-term endeavor. Balance does not mean spending exactly one-fourth of each day on your four priorities; rather, it is recognizing which priorities need attention at a time, and devoting how much attention is necessary without losing sight of the other things that matter.

Mantra:

I live my life in harmony, balancing
my priorities and desires.

Question: What, if anything, might I need to change to create greater harmony in my life?

6
Grit

Grit is the value of rugged, unyielding persistence. Grit is where passion and perseverance meet. Grit will pursue its ends with tireless determination, bounce back quickly from any setback, and continue on its path until we achieve our goal.

Each of the components of Grit are easy to find. Passion is not common, but neither is it rare — most people care deeply about something. Perseverance, likewise, can be found in many individuals and is a worthy trait. When the two are combined though, a certain magic happens and gives rise to Grit: an irresistible force that endures whatever life throws at it, moving even seemingly immovable obstacles. Grit cares so much about what it is doing that it will break down any barrier, fail a thousand times, and simply not quit.

If Grit is one of your core values, then you lived through 2020! Through the series of historic events that tested the mettle of even the sternest among us; Grit pulled you through. If you accomplished more and bounced back faster than those around you, you may count yourself among those with (dare I say it) True Grit.

Mantra:

My passion sets my course, and my perseverance
gets me to my destination.

Question: How can my grit support and inspire others to overcome adversity and achieve their goals?

7
Humor

Humor is the value of laughing until tears roll down your face. Humor can see the funny and silly side of any situation. Humor loves to laugh and is quick to make a joke. At its best, it is a relief and a comfort in even the most difficult of situations. At its worst, it cannot stop giggling, even at a shareholder's meeting or at a funeral. Mind you, this is not necessarily a bad thing, although others in the room may not appreciate it!

Humor's lightness and quick wit almost always help a situation more than they hurt. Many — perhaps most of us are too serious, too much of the time, and that friend who makes us laugh can help us return to our perspective. Humor reminds us of the absurdity of the world and lets us shake off the doom and gloom. Humor can be a wonderful icebreaker, a way to reveal others' "soft spots." Laughter relaxes us and helps us let our guard down, and can be a wonderful catalyst to build relationships.

Humor can have a dark side though, when it seeks a laugh at someone else's expense. Sarcastic humor can be a mask that hides bitterness or despair, and biting humor can do actual harm to the feelings of those who find themselves the butt of the joke. The best humor is that which inspires genuine belly laughs from everyone in the room.

If Humor is a core value for you, you use it for serious stuff! Your clever wit helps you get what you need. You use it effectively to negotiate, gain agreement, and solve problems. If most people who know you describe you as "funny," or you often gather an audience when you tell funny stories, that's a sign that Humor is one of yours.

Mantra:

I see the humor in every aspect of life.

Question: Do I ever make jokes that may be hurtful to others? How can I use humor in a way that is always inclusive and kind, but still just as funny?

8

Trust

The value of Trust aligns with the value of good Relationships. To trust someone is to hold them to a very high standard of behavior — that they will be honest with you, not withhold critical information, respect your boundaries and beliefs, and relate to you consistently whether you are present or absent.

Trust is fundamental to many relationships, especially in our fast-paced and highly connected world, where so much of our sensitive information is so easily uncovered and shared. If you didn't trust your bank, surely you would not keep your money there! And if you didn't trust your spouse, you would be in a constant state of agitation whenever they weren't by your side. If only because distrust is so stressful, most of us choose to trust others until it gives us a reason not to. Of course, when our trust is betrayed, it can be painful or possibly devastating. Even for those who do not have trust as a core value, the relationships most valuable to us tend to be those with the people we most deeply trust.

Trust keeps its promises. It acts in the best interests of others and believes others will do likewise. Trust believes in boundaries and privacy. Ironically, Trust may not always tell the truth — but the choice to withhold truth is motivated by a protective, rather than a deceptive instinct.

When Trust is one of your core values, you choose transparency and honesty over silence or deception. You can respect boundaries and keep secrets. You may be selective in building relationships, and you know that those closest to you will have your back no matter what happens. You work hard to be trustworthy, and trust is an essential foundation underlying your relationships with those who matter most to you.

Mantra:

I trust others and others trust me.

Question: Where can I be more trusting? Where might my trust be misplaced?

9
Gratitude

Especially in America, constant messages bombard us about what we do not have. The message is to buy more, do more, want more, never be satisfied. There is nothing wrong with aspiring, but if it leads to feelings of emptiness, longing, or inadequacy, it does not serve us well.

Those who embrace the value of Gratitude are not consumed with greed or need. Instead, they make a daily practice of appreciating what they have. They are thankful for their capacities, talents, health, family and friends. They appreciate people simply for being themselves, and for all their inherent goodness. They appreciate seeing people help each other, even when simply observing an interaction from the outside. They have a unique ability to be present, to recognize the beauty of each moment, exactly as it is.

Gratitude amplifies positivity. In times of challenge, when it feels difficult to find joy or happiness, often we can still find gratitude. The simple practice of focusing on our gratitude can pull us up when we are feeling down.

If Gratitude is one of your core values, you are probably naturally thankful. An easy test of whether Gratitude is one of your core values is to do this simple exercise: make a list of 100 things you are grateful for right now. Is it easy for you to do? Why or why not?

Mantra:

I easily connect to those things for which I am grateful.

Question: How can I express my gratitude in ways that lift me up and inspire others?

10
Forgiveness

The value of Forgiveness is about understanding that we comprise as much of what we let go, and of what we hold on to. It may appear that forgiving someone for their actions is a gift we give to them. In fact, it is a gift we give to ourselves. When someone values Forgiveness, they do not hold grudges, and they choose to remove spite from their mindset. When you honor the essential humanity of everyone you meet, you can more easily accept the inevitability of mistakes, and give the benefit of the doubt unless there is some compelling reason to do otherwise. And when mistakes occur, forgiveness offers a way forward — to learn from what has occurred, and do better next time.

The way other people choose to think and act is about them, not about you. To believe otherwise is to assign yourself too much significance in someone else's mind. You are important, but not more important than others. In his book The Four Agreements, Don Miguel Ruiz tells us, "don't take anything personally." Forgiveness is the value of knowing when not to take it personally.

When Forgiveness is one of your core values, you are quick to forgive, but not to forget. You may choose to align yourself with those who act authentically and seek to better themselves. You know this pursuit is difficult and will lead to mistakes, and for this reason, you can easily put those mistakes aside and keep moving forward. You recognize your humanity and your fallibility, and you forgive as you hope you will be forgiven — quickly, easily, and with kindness and compassion.

Mantra:

I am open to forgive.

Question: Is there anywhere in my life where I am holding a grudge? What would it take for me to let it go?

11
Frivolity

Given the apparent seriousness of the values considered up to this point, Frivolity may seem a bit out of place. But perhaps that is its purpose? Frivolity — the ability to lighten up, to celebrate, to laugh, to let your hair down (if you have any) enhances the joy of life.

As we age, we risk losing the childlike sense of wonder that drove our every waking move when we were young. Kids laugh easily, as much as they can. They play. They are un-self conscious in their enthusiasm for life. They bounce back from hurt, both physical and emotional, almost as quickly as the hurt happens. They communicate their emotions freely (if you want them to!) and thus release their frustrations rather than keeping them bottled up. Adulthood seems to snuff out the beautiful spark we have as children. To reignite it requires that we choose to get out of our heads and back into our hearts. Many messages we see as adults suggest we are not supposed to be frivolous; that we are failing at "adulting" if we have too much fun. Nonsense! Fun, play, and silliness inspire our creativity and imagination, enabling us to face the day with greater enthusiasm and an ability to solve problems in new ways.

When Frivolity is one of your core values, you understand

how play and childlike wonder help you handle adult situations. You aren't afraid to laugh and dance as if no one is watching. You have seen how fun can make difficult situations easier, and how fearless creativity can solve seemingly intractable problems.

> **Mantra:**
>
> The world is my playground!

Question: What's going on in my life that I am taking too seriously?

12
Vacation

This might seem like an odd item to include in a list of values, but if you think about it, it makes perfect sense. Many people, especially Americans are "workaholics," spending 60 hours or more each week at the office. If we are honest though, we acknowledge we aren't especially efficient during much of that time. Stress, poor diet and sleep habits, and simple exhaustion turn us into "work zombies." Yes, our bodies are sitting at our desks, but our minds are somewhere else entirely.

The solution is Vacation! We need to get away from our routine. When you take a vacation, you can enjoy new experiences that remind you to pay attention to the present moment. You can relax and simply be where you are. Even if you can't jet off to an exotic destination, you can take a Vacation by trying a new restaurant, visiting a nearby park or trail, camping out in your backyard, or just turning off all your electronics and enjoying an "unplugged" day with your favorite snack, beverage and a great book. Vacation, whether you take it at home or thousands of miles away, is a time for exploring your dreams and indulging your senses. You return with new energy, once again ready to dive in and get things done.

If Vacation is one of your core values, you might follow

the philosophy: "Work hard, play hard!" You know that when you take regular opportunities to rejuvenate and experience a change of scenery, you are more focused and more productive in your day-to-day life. You might have a long list of places you want to visit. Planning and scheduling your vacation time is a priority for you, and if your job's paid leave program is "use it or lose it" you've never lost so much as a minute!

Mantra:

I live my best life when I can change
my scenery often.

Question: Where am I, or is someone I know, in a rut? How can I change the scenery?

13
Continuity

Continuity is the value of repeating what works. As we gain experience through the course of our lives, if we are wise we hold on to the lessons we learn and incorporate them into our future endeavors. If something works, we keep doing it. If something doesn't work, we let go of it. When we have momentum on a project, we do whatever we can to keep that momentum going.

The value of Continuity recognizes the importance of recording and communicating what we know. When we learn something of value or use, we pass the knowledge to others. Why make the same mistake twice, or doom others to making the mistakes you have made, when you can remember, record, and share your lessons? Continuity is the value of building a legacy of knowledge, wisdom, and repeatable processes to benefit everyone who comes after you.

Continuity loves a predictable routine. Those who value Continuity may not be the aggressive strivers or adventurous risk-takers, but their steady reliability can be a safe harbor in a turbulent world.

When Continuity is one of your core values, you write things down. You appreciate and learn from the wisdom of others, put systems and processes in place where you can, and take active steps to close knowledge gaps among your colleagues. You have made certain that even when you can't be personally on hand, the information most critical to those around you is still available to them.

Mantra:

Steady as I go.

Question: How can I best help those who rely on my wisdom and my record-keeping?

14
Spirit

"We've got spirit, yes we do! We've got spirit, how 'bout you?" Yes, Spirit is the value of the natural-born cheerleaders. It is a feeling of joie de vivre that permeates and radiates from people who have it. Such people live joyfully, with unfaltering enthusiasm for everything and everyone that matters to them.

Spirit is the value of high engagement. It is leadership through charisma, drawing people toward its light, and encouraging them to become involved in something bigger than themselves. Spirited people LOVE what they do, and their love of what they do is infectious. Spirit is not just a fan; it is a fanatic!

Spirit is best when it is shared. It generates enthusiasm for a shared cause, team, or project. It reflects a commonality of purpose that inspires people to do things together that are bigger than they could do alone. Spirit profoundly believes in a vision, shares it, and amplifies it. If you watched the last game of the 2016 World Series, when the Chicago Cubs won for the first time in 107 years, you saw a spectacular show of Spirit by their fans.

If you have Spirit as a core value, you are a source of boundless energy. You love to go "all in" on whatever you do, and your natural enthusiasm for your work draws the interest and support of others. Whatever you are doing, you and everyone around you are having a great time doing it because of you.

Mantra:

Let's go Mets! (well, Okay, that's my mantra.
You might want to write your own.)

Question: Where in my life is some cheerleading needed?

15
Faith

Faith happens when belief joins constancy. It is unfaltering in the face of uncertainty. Faith, when fully realized, is nearly immune to doubt — it trusts in what it believes, and never wavers.

Faith focuses on something or someone. You may have Faith in yourself; I hope you do! You may have Faith in the Universe, a religious path, sacred text, or a higher power. You may have Faith in an institution or a process, and trust that it will keep working as it should. You may have Faith in family members, friends, or other people who guide you on your life's journey. You may have Faith in your vision, purpose, and values. You may have Faith in these things — perhaps all the time or at different times.

Can you imagine how it would be if you took the time to make a list of your values and you did not believe and have Faith in them? Would they actually guide your behavior, or just be words on the wall — an engraved plaque of pretty but meaningless text? Don Miguel Ruiz, in his book, The Four Agreements, says to "be impeccable with your word." When you don't have Faith in your words, they are not very impeccable, are they?

If Faith is a core value for you, there's a good chance you've lived through times of significant doubt or challenge, and the people or things in which you have Faith have endured for you. You do not follow blindly; rather, you have experienced challenges that the object of your Faith has overcome, and you have embraced completely the truth that this experience has revealed to you.

Mantra:

I am steadfast in my faith.

Question: When did I last evaluate the truths in which I have placed my faith? What beliefs do I find difficult to defend when they are challenged, and what do I want to do about it?

16
Friendship

To value our Friends is to appreciate how other people enrich our lives when we allow them to grow close to us. A group of friends working together can achieve far more than any of them could do alone. A group of friends playing, laughing, or relaxing together can lift each other's spirits as nothing else can.

Friendship shows up in our lives in many ways. We have favorite coworkers who enjoy lunches or happy hours together, laughing and providing welcome breaks from the daily grind. We have neighbors who went above and beyond for us when the cat got out, or a tree fell on a power line. And we have people who, for whatever reason, become beloved members of our chosen family.

Our Friends accompany us through life's ups and downs. They applaud us when we are successful and comfort us when we are struggling. They double our joy and divide our sorrow, as the saying goes. In sharing our lives with our friends, we deepen our human experience and expand our understanding of all the ways love manifests in the world.

When Friendship is one of your core values, you prioritize quality over quantity in your relationships. You probably have a few friends who are the most important people in your life, and you are a loyal and steadfast friend. If one of your friends truly needs you, you will serve them in any way you can, without hesitation, and they know they can count on you.

Mantra:

I cherish the time I spend with my friends.

Question: What qualities do I value most in my closest friends? How might I emulate those qualities?

17
Truth

Obi-Wan Kenobi wisely said, "many of the truths we cling to depend greatly on our own point of view." Truth is the value of seeking that which transcends fact and opinion and feels deeply right.

Truth connects to honesty (value number 18 in this book), but not always to "correctness" by someone else's standards or definitions. You may feel or speak something that feels like Truth to you, and when you do so, you are honest and authentic, whether anyone else's opinion or even their fact is consistent with it. Your Truth and my Truth are different, and that's fine!

Truth is unshakeable, and that can be a precious thing. To stand firm by your Truth can be honorable. And, it can also be a blind spot or even dangerous, if you deny objective evidence or facts that disrupt your beliefs. Take care to remember: "you are entitled to your opinions, but not to your facts."

If Truth is a core value, strive to live by it. Internal consistency is important to you. You search tirelessly to understand what is right and what is wrong, and while you adhere faithfully to the Truth you know, you understand that because it "depends on your point of view," you are open to change and growth as you uncover new and deeper layers of Truth.

Mantra:

I fearlessly live my truth.

Question: How can I show empathy and respect for those whose truth differs from mine?

18
Honesty

Honesty is the value of telling the truth, all the time, no matter what. It rejects the notion of "white lies" — there are no "good" or "safe" or "justifiable" forms of lying. Honesty means being truthful with yourself and to others. It requires not only that we do not speak untruths but also that we speak the truth even when it would be easier to remain silent. Honesty does not tolerate lies of omission any more than it tolerates lies of commission.

Honesty is perhaps the most uncompromising of all the values. Either you are honest, or you are not. Even the act of justifying an exception to a policy of being honest is dishonest! Perhaps this is why it is common to hear the words "brutal" and "honest" together. Many people and organizations claim they value honesty, but if pressed, they will confess to having told "little" lies many times. So if you claim to value honesty, ask yourself: "are you REALLY being honest? REALLY?"

If Honesty is one of your core values, being truthful and trustworthy is paramount for you. You speak the truth, even when it hurts. You expect others to be honest with you. You would rather someone be honest than polite, and you will choose truth over diplomacy if diplomacy would require dishonesty. Just remember, when you need to be brutally honest, that the world needs more Honesty, but perhaps a little less brutality!

Mantra:

I am honest with myself and others
no matter the consequences.

Question: Do I always need to say what I think? When might silence be kinder or less harmful than speaking the truth?

19
Charity

I n the Bible, Paul writes to the Corinthians of three values — Faith, Hope, and Charity, noting that "the greatest of these is Charity." This particular Bible was passed down in Greek, and the Greek word for this is $\alpha\gamma\alpha\pi\varepsilon$, which means "universal love" or selfless love of strangers, nature, or God. Charity is the value of selfless giving.

Charity drives us to help those in need, to give whatever we can spare, and sometimes even a little more than that. Charity can take the form of financial or material giving, or giving volunteer time. Often, but not always, people practice Charity toward a specific purpose, organization, or cause important to them. Or we are moved in generous ways to respond to those afflicted by a world event such as a natural disaster or pandemic disease. The practice of Charity is an active and visible expression of love.

If you have Charity as a core value, you respond with action when you witness hardship or injustice. You look for ways to serve and support those who are struggling, whether it be people facing poverty, illness, or disaster; neglected or abused animals; threats to ecosystems or even people facing barriers to greater opportunity. Your generosity and compassion travel hand in hand, moving you to be constantly looking out for ways to ease suffering and make the world a better place.

The caveat of Charity is "giving until it hurts." My friend Chris Sopa likes to say, "I cannot give what I do not have," a glorious reminder to, as they say on the airplane, "put your own oxygen mask on first." Your generosity is needed in the world, and equally important is preserving your capacity to be generous in the future.

Mantra:

I generously help those in need.

Question: How can I best balance my own needs with those of others?

20
Action

Action is the value that moves us to roll up our sleeves and get to work! Action is a tireless and restless value that wants to get moving once the plan is in place. Action reminds us that even when we aren't producing at top efficiency, it is better to do something than to do nothing.

While it is important to dream, plan, organize, and think things through, we can realize nothing until we take Action.

We must do the things on the to-do list to achieve our goals and manifest our dreams. Sometimes we have to keep going even when we'd rather take a break. Marathon runners are pretty tired at the halfway point, but they keep going. Action is the value that motivates us to start the race in the first place, and then to keep putting one foot in front of the other until we cross the finish line.

If Action is a core value for you, you are a doer! You love to make progress on projects, get balls rolling, see things moving, get things done. Checking things off your list is one highlight of your day. Other people love you for your energy and your determination. Just watch out for two things: one, don't let other people take advantage of you and let you do more than your share. Two, remember that being busy is not the same as being productive. Make sure you know what you are seeking to accomplish with your Action.

Mantra:

I get things done!

Question: Do I spend enough time planning, prioritizing, or clarifying my goals before taking action? Could I save myself time, energy, or re-work if I took a bit of extra effort to plan?

21
Rest

Most books and articles about leadership and success talk about hard work, persistence, and decisive action being the best way to achieve your goals. And certainly, those things are necessary, and even expressed as values in this book. The surest way to burn yourself out and ultimately get nowhere is to beat yourself unrelentingly against your to-do list. Every bit as important as the Action, is the Rest.

There is a reason our labor laws mandate periodic breaks during the workday. To function effectively, efficiently, and safely, we need to step away from the desk or the assembly line for a few minutes and take a breather. Athletes understand the importance of "tapering" before a race and "recovering" afterwards. The stress of exercise literally breaks the fibers of your muscles. You must give your body time to repair that damage to gain strength.

Mental activity, too, is stressful and requires recovery time. Have you ever been "stuck" on a problem that refused to yield to your most intense attention, only to have a brilliant solution come to you when you wake up from a good night's sleep? These moments serve as a reminder that your subconscious brain can process thousands of times more information than your conscious brain. Rest allows the subconscious brain the time and space it needs to help you uncover your brilliance.

Our bodies and minds are a bit like rechargeable batteries. We work well, but we only have so many hours of functional time before we need to take a break and recharge. Rest is the value of recognizing that taking that recharging time is critical to our ability to harness our full capacity.

If Rest is one of your core values, you understand that your "downtime" determines your "uptime." You build breaks into your workdays, and you know the value of taking "mental health days" and regular vacations. You know that when you're struggling to solve problems or come up with ideas, sometimes the best thing to do is let it go for a while and come back to it later. You're not lazy, but you know that a good night's sleep is a gift and the occasional nap hurts nobody.

Mantra:

I make time for downtime.

Question: Do I ever mistake procrastination for rest? What might I be putting off, or taking longer to accomplish, in the name of rest?

22
Intensity

Intensity is the value of being "all in." When you approach something with Intensity, you focus absolutely on that thing, and you are giving it everything you've got. Your energy is palpable and contagious. Your singular devotion to your mission lights you up until you glow like the sun.

Intensity allows you to fixate on a task or a problem. It lets you block out every distraction and enter the state of "flow" where time seems to stand still and the work you are doing seems effortless. You may not even notice if there are other people around you, but if they are present, they will find your energy irresistible and feel compelled to help and support you.

When Intensity focuses on another person, it is heady stuff indeed! Both you and that other person will feel as though you are the only two living things in existence: absorbed and consumed in each other's presence. When this comes from a loving place, it is exhilarating and breathtaking, almost unbearably wonderful. When it comes from a place of fear or anger, it is terrifying and awful. Take care with your Intensity — it has the power to harm and the power to heal.

If Intensity is one of your core values, you are, well, intense! You have a nearly limitless ability to focus on one thing with every ounce of your being. You probably work best when you can get completely immersed in something with no distractions, and you know how to set up your work environment to minimize interruptions. You might be a "weekend warrior," able to write a report or remodel a bathroom in a day or two of furious effort. Be mindful of how people are responding to you — Intensity can trigger a "deer in the headlights" response from some people.

Mantra:

I go all in, and I go all out!

Question: Where can I focus more intently on something important to me? Where might I need to back off a bit?

23
Fairness

Fairness is the value that seeks justice in the world. Its mission is to serve all people in accordance with their individual circumstances and needs. Fairness is sometimes mistaken for equality, but they are different things.

Suppose a company occupies a ten-story building, and the break room is on the second floor, and everyone is given a ten-minute break at the same time each morning. Those who work on the second floor take a leisurely walk to the break room and enjoy a cup of coffee before returning to their desks. But for those on the top three floors of the building, simply getting to the break room takes six or seven minutes! All are given an equal break. But is it fair?

Fairness acknowledges that there are winners and losers if the rules have been followed and the participants are gracious; that's Okay. Fairness does not insist that everyone receive a "participation award", but advocates for equality of opportunity. Only the fastest runner will win the race, but everyone should have the chance to run.

Fairness accounts for individual differences and unique situations. It looks for ways to level the playing field so that all feel included and valued. It cannot abide a world where some are privileged while others are made to struggle. Its voice is not itself loud, but it demands that all other voices be heard.

If you have fairness as a core value, you are careful to consider each person's voice and needs. You are incensed by any injustice, whether it be political, social, or personal. You will defend those who are weaker or meeker and chastise those who abuse power. You admire those who show exceptional fair play and servant leadership.

Mantra:

I treat people as they wish to be treated.

Question: Am I fair in all areas of my life? Do I have any blind spots around fairness or fair treatment of others?

24
Love

My personal bias will reveal itself here, as Love is my number one value. Love is the pinnacle of human experience, the ultimate expression of care, the highest good we may strive for.

Love is a value, and Love is a verb. Love expresses itself in what we do for other people. It can manifest in various ways, and indeed other languages have different words for the varied forms of Love. Value 19, Charity, is one form of Love — the Love of strangers and the desire to serve humanity. Value 3, Passion, is another form of Love, especially when directed toward another individual. Love often, but not always, has an object, and when it does, we feel compelled to admire and serve it in any way we can.

If you are lucky enough to have a healthy relationship with a partner, Love is about being enmeshed in that other person. It moves you to serve them and support them in any way you can, so that they can become their best selves. And in that process, you become your best self.

Ultimately, however Love plays out for you, you will know it when you find yourself feeling, speaking, and doing good. True joy and deep gratitude will come naturally, and the energy that emanates from you will spread that joy and gratitude around.

When Love is a core value, you may feel almost as though you need nothing else in your life. You may be "in Love" with another person, with many people, with cultures, hobbies, institutions — being engrossed in what you Love fills you up in a way that supersedes such trifles as food, water, or sleep. You do not lightly say "I Love you," but when you do say it, you mean it with all your heart.

Mantra:

I love without reservation.

Question: How can I express love more fully? Who needs to know, right now, that I love them?

25
Duty

Duty is the value of those who serve. For those called to Duty, the mission is clear. Some purpose, cause, or ideal lays a foundation for what must be done, and Duty steps forward to take on the challenge.

Duty is an altruistic calling, and one that follows a "rule book." Duty is devoted to its cause and will pursue its purpose tirelessly, regardless of how arduous the task before it. Deep commitment and loyalty to the cause gives Duty the strength to serve, and the courage to persevere no matter the obstacles.

Duty is a double-edged sword. When aligned to a noble cause, Duty is heroic and fearless. But Duty can also be dangerous when it blindly follows a leader or belief that may be detrimental to self or others. Many soldiers have fought and died for a cause history has shown to be misguided. When loyalty to a demagogue, an unscrupulous friend, or a toxic marriage partner leads us to behave in ways that harm ourselves or others, Duty is not serving us well.

If you consider Duty to be one of your core values, you see the needs of others as a greater good than your personal comfort. Your loyalty to a cause is unmatched, and you show it in your actions. When you believe in a mission, people know they can count on you to be the first to arrive on the scene, and the last to leave.

Mantra:

I am a faithful servant.

Question: What causes deserve more dutiful attention from me right now? Where might my sense of duty be misplaced or detrimental to my well-being or that of others?

26
Honor

Honor holds the self to the highest of standards. It is the value of absolute respect for oneself, another person, an idea, or an ideal. It expects impeccable conduct in word and deed. Honor demands that its adherents be trustworthy and willing to sacrifice for others or for the greater good. Honor is a value of integrity, aligned with good. It follows a strict code of conduct — and does so with eyes wide open. There is no blind faith in Honor. It has carefully considered its beliefs and loyalties and chosen its path with intention.

Honor is a reverent value, sometimes so serious as to elicit teasing or laughter from those who don't understand the deep sincerity from which it springs. Marvel Comics fans will remember Thor's oft-repeated axiom concerning his magical hammer, Mjölnir, that is impossibly heavy to lift except by a very few chosen heroes: "It is not about strength. It is about worthiness." Honor is the value of worthiness.

The other side of the Honor coin is self-righteousness. Honor may react badly to a challenge or insult, or harshly judge those who do not have it as a core value. When Honor carries too far, it can alienate others.

If Honor is one of your core values, people depend on you to do the right thing every time, and you rarely, if ever, disappoint them. If you do, it tears you up — Honor can be an unforgiving mistress. You are a fast friend and a defender of truth, and the world needs more like you. Remember though, to give yourself grace. You are still human, and not every hill requires you to die on it. It is important to find the balance between pride and humility, and between heroism and humanness.

Mantra:

I am a person of honor.

Question: How can I be compassionate when my honor is challenged?

27
Invincibility

Invincibility is the value of feeling unable to be defeated. Invincibility is tireless, relentless, and nearly immune to the challenges it faces. Invincibility says, "never give up, never surrender."

And if you recognize those words as quotes from the movie Galaxy Quest, you'll also notice that Invincibility, like Honor, can be so serious that it becomes comical. Its absolute commitment to success will break down walls, bust through glass ceilings, leap tall buildings in a single bound... you get the idea. "Failure is not an option" for those who hold Invincibility as a core value. And while those who treat their goals with less monumental gravitas may find Invincibility hard to take seriously, Invincibility is undeterred. Skepticism is just one more barrier to break down in the dogged pursuit of success. You'll notice that when you succeed, the people you left in the dust won't be laughing anymore.

Invincibility has a blind spot: it overlooks any vulnerability or flaw in its plans. All things have some degree of fragility, no matter how solid they appear. A bit of attention to this can make all the difference when circumstances force you to implement "Plan B" on your way to your goal.

If you have Invincibility as a core value you will ultimately succeed in any task, goal or project to which you apply your efforts. However much energy, time, or dedication is required, you will invest it, and your effort will pay off. It's wise to check in with yourself every so often to make certain your goal is still worthwhile to you. Relentlessness in the pursuit of a goal can turn into a grim determination to finish the job, even after the reasons to do it have faded. Why stay on a project or in a situation beyond the point where you are receiving value or benefit from it? Thankless tasks are exactly that; your fierce focus is best invested in those activities that give you true joy and satisfaction.

Mantra:

When I decide to achieve a goal,
my success is inevitable.

Question: What makes my goals worth relentlessly pursuing?

28
Cunning

Cunning may seem like a curious value to include. It sometimes carries an unfriendly connotation, as though it means some harm to those it outwits. But Cunning need not be an adversarial trait. There is great value in the kind of ingenuity that travels with Cunning.

The Cunning value is sly like a fox. It possesses keen street smarts and sharp wit. It is a trickster, but not necessarily in a mean-spirited or manipulative way. It is clever, wily, nimble and quick on the uptake. It is seldom caught by surprise, but it is quite capable of surprising others. At its best, such surprises are a cause of great delight — never expected but appreciated for their thoughtful planning and innovative execution.

As with all values, Cunning can have a dark side when taken to extremes. When Cunning seeks to deceive or manipulate, it will not welcome its surprises. Cunning can do great harm when practiced without care.

If you hold Cunning as one of your core values, you are always aware of your options. You can plan meticulously, but you can just as easily improvise, and you are rarely caught with your guard down. Yours is the unorthodox but ingenious solution to the problem others can't seem to solve. You have a knack for sensing which direction the wind is blowing, and a talent for adjusting your sails to outpace every other boat in the water, whether or not you actually entered the race. People describe you with words like "sharp" and "clever", and they appreciate the way you keep them on their toes.

Mantra:

I am the sharpest knife in the drawer.

Question: What aspect(s) of my life could benefit from an ingenious plan right now?

29
Heart

Heart is the value of dogs and underdogs — an earnest, unconditional capacity for caring and a desire to gain acceptance. Different from love, Heart represents the capacity to love and to have empathy. It is warm, sincere, and guileless. It gives of itself freely, expecting nothing in return. When you encounter Heart, you like it instinctively.

Heart is the hallmark of Hallmark Channel Original Movies. It shows up on greeting cards and in feel-good stories of reunions between lonely people and long-lost pets. It is the against-all-odds Little League team winning the big game, and "if you build it, they will come." It gives us a warm glow and perhaps chokes us up just a little. Most of us resist it even though we love how it makes us feel, because Heart is only available to us when we are willing to be vulnerable.

Heart is the value of the empath. They are generous, gentle souls and for that reason, they can be vulnerable to hurt. Many people are afraid of this vulnerability, and shield themselves with cynicism or mocking when they see Heart. It's easy to take advantage of, or to drain from, a person with Heart.

If Heart is one of your core values, you are that rare person who is not afraid to open yourself up to genuine caring. You are naturally warm, kind, sincere — if someone compares you to Mr. Rogers, they flatter you. Your friends and family know they can come to you when they are hurting, and you will know just what to say or do to make them feel better. And you love it when the good guys win the day.

Mantra:

I fearlessly reveal my heart
and share my compassion.

Question: Are there places in my life where I'm withholding my heart? What would be different if I opened up?

30
Pride

Pride is the value of ownership of the self. It can be a tricky one to navigate, being also called one of the seven deadly sins. Too little Pride, and your efforts and accomplishments feel meaningless; too much, and you become a legend in your own mind.

When in perfect balance, Pride finds joy both in the self's achievements and those of others.

It recognizes all the things that deserve recognition: goals achieved, skills acquired, projects completed, milestones reached. Pride often comes with loyalty, as with "school spirit" or patriotism. In balance however, it never tips over into fanaticism or tribalism. It recognizes the worthiness of the opponent in a fair competition. Pride loves to win, but it is a gracious winner and also a gracious loser. Pride can say, "may the best person win" and mean it. It is confident in the belief that all those who have the courage to enter the competition are the best, each in their way. Of course, Pride's greatest moments are those when "our side" reigns victorious. The accomplishments of those we love will spark our Pride.

When Pride is one of your core values, you are secure in yourself and take full ownership of your strengths, skills, and talents. You know that time invested in enhancing your strengths is time well spent, and you can readily relate to my friend Jay Niblick's mantra: "If it's not my genius, it's not my job." You also recognize that the achievements and talents of others, especially those closest to you, are worthy to be celebrated.

Mantra:

I own my talents, skills, and successes,
and celebrate my victories.

Question: What is true in my life that I am not proud of? What do I want to change about it?

31
Self

To value the Self is to recognize the essential wisdom of my friend Chris Sopa's reminder: "I cannot give what I do not have." Self is engaged in a lifelong journey that it knows to be right. As with many other values, it must find a balance. Too little sense of Self, and we become doormats before the wants and whims of others. Too much, and we become vain and blind to others' needs.

As a value, Self "puts its mask on first." It is mindful of all its needs — body, mind, and spirit, and seeks a center of wholeness and wellness from which it can expand out to serve the world. Self is confidence without arrogance. It practices the principle of "enlightened self-interest," recognizing that healthy interdependence among all people and all things is the best way to get its own needs fully met.

If Self is one of your core values, you have a deep knowledge of your strengths, potential, and needs. You are comfortable setting boundaries to ensure that your well-being is a top priority. You take excellent care of yourself — you are likely in excellent health (or, if not, you may manage a chronic illness or disability effectively). You know that if you put yourself first, you are in the best possible place to serve and support others.

When Self is a core value, beware of becoming self-obsessed — not in the sense of being narcissistic, but in the sense of turning too far inward, constantly self-analyzing, reading every self-help book, losing yourself in "finding yourself." Navel-gazing can serve a purpose, but only to a point.

Mantra:

Loving myself is my first step in serving the world.

Question: How do I balance my focus on myself whilst making connections with others?

32
Camaraderie

Camaraderie is the value of esprit de corps. (I couldn't resist using a French phrase to define a French word!) Camaraderie knows that no person is an island, and that when a group of people get together and work effectively as a team, they can achieve so much more than any of them could ever do alone. Indeed, a team of four people with great Camaraderie may accomplish the work of eight people or more, with less individual effort and far more fun!

Camaraderie is a trusting value, one of active involvement. A group that has Camaraderie supports each other in working toward a shared vision — none of this nonsense where one member does all the work while the others watch! The group's members have a deep commitment to one another's growth. Camaraderie knows that success encompasses both the achievement of the group's vision and each individual's happiness and wellbeing.

It might seem like Camaraderie is just teamwork — but it's more than that. A team that has Camaraderie is not always the winning team, but it is the team that had the most fun doing the job. Teamwork may win the game, but Camaraderie goes out for a beer afterwards even if they lose.

You'll know Camaraderie is a core value for you if you

are a natural team player, preferring group work over solo efforts. Others recognize you as a cheerleader of teams and groups, fostering healthy communication and trust. When you are on a team, the work doesn't feel like work. You love nothing more than being on a great team, and others will want to be on yours!

Mantra:

I love it when I'm with my team.

Question: Where do I see teamwork without camaraderie, and how can I help infuse more fun?

33
Simplicity

The world is a complex place. A staggering quantity of information continuously bombards us, and "stuff" exists in infinite variety, competing for our attention at every moment. The value of Simplicity says, "enough is enough!" Simplicity has what it needs and forgoes what it does not. It seeks to eliminate complexity and excess wherever possible, using only what is necessary and sufficient.

Simplicity is the value of small words and short sentences, seeking to be understood quickly and easily. Using fewer items, taking less time, and completing a task in fewer steps are the goals of Simplicity.

If Simplicity is one of your core values, you know the importance of prioritizing what matters most to you and eliminating the fluff. You might be a minimalist, but not necessarily. Even if not though, you probably have little use for big houses or a lot of possessions, and you despise needless waste. Your ideal environment is tidy and clean, and your ideal workflow includes only the essential steps.

Mantra:

Less is more.

Question: Where in my life do I find clutter or unnecessary complexity? What if anything, do I want to do about it? Is there anything in my life that is too simple, or would benefit by being a bit more fleshed out?

34
Competition

If the idea of "participation awards" disgusts you, you may value Competition. As a value, Competition loves to win and is not interested in second place. It strives endlessly, constantly comparing itself against others and against ideals. It seeks to beat its personal best and dreams of breaking records. It will use every resource at its disposal to succeed.

Competition is a motivator beyond a simple desire to win. When Competition sees its name on a list, it wants to be at the top. Competition wants the nicest house, the best car, the most attractive spouse, the highest achieving kids. If there is a way to be better than others, Competition is already on the way there.

Competition is virtuous in the company of sportsmanship. It can become a vice in the company of brinkmanship. The desire to win is healthy until it turns into the desire for others to lose.

If Competition is one of your core values, you are likely (but not necessarily) an athlete and/or a sports fan. Games, sports, races, any form of Competition may draw your interest, and you probably prefer to do things you are good at. You love to win and hate to lose, and may sometimes imagine that something is a Competition when it is not.

Remember to be a good sport, gracious in victory and defeat, and be aware of those who don't share your love for Competition. Harness this value to excel in the pursuits you are passionate about, and you will always be a winner.

Mantra:

I live for the thrill of rising above the rest.

Question: In what circumstances can my competitive spirit best serve me, and when it does not, how can I use cooperation and consensus building to help everyone win?

35
Celebration

Celebration is the value of marking moments with joyful intention. Celebration leaves no holiday, no achievement, no milestone untouched by acknowledgment, excitement, and probably cake! The value of Celebration embraces the ritual around life events, relishing each birthday, each award ceremony, and every special moment as a perfect excuse for a party. It is a value of savoring the extraordinary, of calling attention to each choice and event that is worthy of being appreciated.

If Celebration is one of your core values, every day is a holiday. You will readily turn any moment, from your team winning the Super Bowl to your child doing well on a math test, into a reason to pull out the noisemakers and go out for ice cream. Your family and friends love the way you make their smallest successes feel like major victories, and you are a ton of fun to be around!

A caveat: it can get to be too much. When Celebrations happen too often, they may stop feeling so special, or it may be tempting to "top" the last one with increasingly extravagant fanfare. Too much Celebration can be expensive, exhausting, and fattening. When you value Celebration in context with other values, though, you know Celebrations are too few for most folks.

When you celebrate your value of Celebration, you help others remember how important it is to infuse every day with joy, fun, and recognition of wins large and small.

Mantra:

I celebrate life's milestones with joy and fanfare.

Question: What's the best way for me to determine how, and how often, to celebrate?

36
Inspiration

The word "Inspiration" literally means, "breathing in." So the value of Inspiration is the value of bringing something into yourself that revitalizes you. The stories and experiences of others drive Inspiration, and seek to drive others with its story. Inspiration is the value of uncovering that which lies within you, because of paying attention to that which is all around you. It loves all things new, to be sure, but also has the wisdom to see familiar things with fresh eyes. It notices, and gains valuable insight from things that others miss or disregard. It has a boundless capacity to make new discoveries and unexpected connections, simply because it is always tuned in to its surroundings.

Inspiration may sound like a big thing, but it can come from the smallest sources. The way the sun dapples through leaves, or the course a dandelion seed takes from its flower, can be inspiring. A symphony can inspire, but so can a single note.

When Inspiration is one of your core values, you find it everywhere. You have a natural sense of what motivates you, and you seek it out in people, places and experiences. You soak up sensory experiences like a sponge, whether savoring an exotic new cuisine or losing track of time exploring a museum. The first time you went on YouTube, your family didn't see you for a week. You probably read Wikipedia for fun. Through it all, you are taking notes, creating connections, making excited phone calls to your friends — "hey, did you know…?" And it is this enchanting wonderment that others love about you (even though they tease you about it, too). To turn this value into a superpower, remember to follow through with the ideas that most excite you. If you can turn an idea into a product, an organization, or a solution to a challenging problem, your Inspiration could become a fulfilling hobby or career that also serves the wider world.

Mantra:

I gratefully receive inspiration from all around me.

Question: When something inspires me, what does it inspire me to do?

37
Creativity

Creativity is the value of applied imagination. Creativity fearlessly experiments with new and interesting ways to do things. It embraces the ideas of others, but puts its own spin on them. It is a messy value, splattered with paint, sticky with glue, joyful in its pursuit of novelty and uniqueness. Creativity has a vibrant picture of the world in its mind's eye, and it is itching to make that picture real. It is ready to learn every tool or technique that it might need to build its colorful utopia, and invent a few of its own if necessary.

Creativity may be a core value for you if you love to make things. And by "things" I don't mean those things that are commonly called "art" or "crafts." Your Creativity could be expressed in writing, cooking, fashion, architecture or construction, child-rearing or even dreaming up a better way to lay out a financial report. The common thread is that you imagine new, better, or simply unconventional ways of doing things, and then try your idea to see if it works. It's the application of your imagination, your willingness to experiment, to fail, to adapt and try again, that marks you as Creative. And if you do this frequently, naturally and by preference, Creativity could be one of your core values. If you're not sure, there's an easy way to check: if other people are always and forever saying "Wow. You are so creative." That's a dead giveaway.

Mantra:

I use my hands, heart and mind to
make the world better and more fun.

Question: What's the best way to capture my creative ideas as I have them, and what tools or techniques can I use to choose my favorites and bring them to fruition?

38
Imagination

" One little spark of inspiration lies at the heart of all creation. Right at the start of everything that's new, one little spark lights up for you." -Richard Sherman

Imagination is the value of boundless thought. Some people talk about "thinking outside the box." Imagination has no idea what this "box" has to do with anything — it has never even seen this box, much less been inside it. Imagination knows there are infinite ways of thinking. It dreams on a grand scale, stretching boundaries, discovering alternatives no one else has considered.

Imagination is pure and playful, like Figment, the Disney character that was created as the original mascot of EPCOT Center when it first opened. Figment is conceived as a figment of your Imagination — an expression of limitless possibility. He is a colorful, mischievous, unconventional rule-breaker who delights in literally turning the world upside down to see it from a different perspective. This is the power of Imagination.

If Imagination is one of your core values, your mind is a playground of possibility. Your daydreams are not limited by what is known or what has been done before. The entire universe is just the right size for your mental meanderings, and you could be ready to go anywhere, and try anything, at the first suggestion of newness or fun.

I hate to put caveats on Imagination, because it is rare and beautiful and fragile, especially in children. But beware of losing yourself in endless dreaming. In the absence of action, Imagination is wasted. Take your wildest dream and turn it into an amazing new reality.

Mantra:

My mind holds limitless possibilities.

Question: What would my wildest dream look like if it existed in real life? Who could help me create or achieve it?

39
Communication

Communication is the value of understanding and being understood through the use of focused listening and clear self-expression. Articulate speech, expressive art and compelling music are some of the many ways that Communication shares its vision with the world. Communication seeks to make connections with others, creating vivid mental images that others easily understand.

Communication as a concept is simple to define but difficult to do well. "Listening" is not just hearing words — it is absorbing and interpreting tone, nuance, body language, and even breathing, to comprehend the full meaning behind the words. "Communicating" is not just saying words, and in fact may not involve words at all — it is expressing oneself in an authentic, truthful way that reveals feelings as much as thoughts. Communication has a clear, complete picture in mind, and can convey it effectively to another person.

If Communication is one of your core values, it's possible that "words of affirmation" are your primary love language. It is important, and also very natural for you to speak, listen, write, or otherwise use a language to make connections with other people. Writing, speaking, or singing might be a major aspect of your professional or personal life. You are probably eloquent, and certainly expressive by nature, and you live for the moments when your words connect with another person.

Mantra:

I love it when I understand and
feel understood by others.

Question: How can I use my voice to lift up important truths and amplify other voices?

40
Presence

Presence is the value of being exactly where you are, fully occupying this precise moment in space and time. It seems simple and obvious, yet it may take years of reflection, coaching and guidance to even understand.

Presence is a total involvement in conversation, viewing of a movie or show, eating a meal, being with a child in their environment — no distractions, no preoccupation with the past or the future, no interruptions. Imagine being in a face-to-face conversation with one other person, without phones ringing, devices buzzing, or 'ooh, let's Google that'; a simple, direct sharing of thoughts and feelings, all in person, and not a screen in sight. Could you handle such a conversation? Presence is a practice of intense focus and concentration, but also one of surrender. It embraces this exact second, with no thought of the past, the future, or even of how the person with you will respond to your communication a moment from now. Presence surrenders itself absolutely to the now, diving into the depths of feeling and understanding that await.

Presence also has the capacity to be completely alone. It can find sublime peace in solitude and meditation. When you can be fully present with yourself, you can see your surroundings, explore your innermost thoughts, and discover ideas that only surface when you can hear the "still, small voice within."

When Presence is one of your core values, you show up for others like no one else can. You are enthralled by what you see before you, taking in every sight, sound, smell, taste and sensation. You don't waste time wondering what could have been, or daydreaming about "some day." You have found a way, as productivity guru David Allen puts it, to "be at peace with what you are NOT doing." You believe in the power of total engagement with each moment and experience, and you naturally attract and are attracted to others who share your ability to be right here, right now.

Mantra:

I am exactly where I need to be at this moment.

Question: How do the other people in my life want me to show up for them?

41
Resourcefulness

Resourcefulness is the value of knowing how to meet your needs. Resourcefulness understands and uses everything available to it, and knows how to get whatever it may lack in a moment. It is well-connected. If Resourcefulness doesn't have the answer, it knows who does. Resourcefulness works effectively with people, tools, processes, and information to overcome obstacles and achieve goals.

Resourcefulness can think of ten different uses for a single item, and ten different items that could be put to the same use. It always has the right tool for the job, and if it doesn't, it can adapt the tools it has to work just as well. Resourcefulness can solve problems no one else can solve, in ways no one else would ever think of. Resourcefulness has fixed the thing before most others even realized it was broken.

If Resourcefulness is one of your core values, people know they can count on you to find answers, solve problems, or connect to people who can help them achieve their goals. You are — and love to be — the "go-to guy" when challenges arise. You are ready for whatever comes your way, able to apply cleverness and creativity to any situation. Just remember; humans work best when they work interdependently. It's good to be self-sufficient, yet it is also important to stay connected to others. It feels great to be needed, but not so great to be used or taken for granted.

Mantra:

I make the best use of all of my resources
to fulfill my needs and serve others.

Question: How can I use my resourcefulness to serve others while also honoring their agency?

42
Renewal

Renewal is the value of recovering from adverse circumstances. It is the tulip bulb that sprouts, grows, blossoms, withers, dies back, lies quietly underground through a long winter, and comes back to do it all again the following year.

Renewal adapts to the changing world. It may need to take a minute to rest, to "lay low" and regenerate after an effortful push. It is not available 100% of the time. But no matter what happens, Renewal reminds us we will recover. We will bounce back. We will come back to life in the following season, bigger, better and more beautiful.

Renewal is energized by beginning, or by beginning again. It is not afraid to make a new start, even if the last start, or the last hundred starts, didn't work out according to plan. Renewal is not afraid of failure or endings because it recognizes the potential for new and wonderful things to emerge from the ashes. Renewal has a deep understanding of the importance of creative destruction — that sometimes, the new can only emerge when the old is dismantled.

Renewal may be one of your core values if you have come through an earth-shattering experience and are better for it. You accept what you can't control and find a source of strength in the possibilities that always come hand in hand with adversity.

Mantra:

I always bounce back.

Question: Who needs your help right now to find the growth opportunity in their struggle?

43
Courage

Courage is the value of feeling fear and doing it anyway. Courage is ready to do whatever it takes to survive, thrive and succeed, even if it might hurt. The word "courage" comes from the Latin word for "heart." Courage goes deeper than mere bravery or boldness, taking leaps of faith and winning against even the most insurmountable odds.

Courage is steadfast in its belief. It will more readily stare down a challenge than back down from it. But it is important to understand that Courage is not the absence of fear. Fearlessness can be foolhardy, taking unnecessary chances. Courage accepts fear as part of the cost of doing business. It does not ignore its fear; instead, it recognizes that other things matter more than fear.

Because Courage understands that life involves risk, Courage chooses its battles wisely. Courage does not seek conflict, nor does it accept an obligation to fight and die on every hill where conflict might occur. Courage comes from the heart, guided to pursue its highest right, undaunted by anything that stands in its way.

Courage may be a core value for you if you have ever imagined yourself as the knight in shining armor. You are willing to take any action necessary in pursuit, or defense, of your beliefs. The world needs you to stand up for those who need and deserve justice and respect, but do not feel brave. And take care not to fall into the trap of the "savior" as that role may rob others of their agency and dignity.

Mantra:

I overcome every obstacle in the pursuit
of my heart's truest desires.

Question: How can I listen more deeply to my heart and tap into my courage in moments of doubt?

44
Curiosity

Curiosity is the value of the tireless explorer. Curiosity constantly seeks new ideas, new information, and new experiences. Curiosity wants to know everything and has endless energy for learning. It is a wide-eyed sense of wonder that is infectious to those around it. It is also a five-year-old with a thousand questions!

Curiosity doesn't just learn something new every day — it learns something new every chance it gets. It wants to know who is doing what, where, when, and how. More importantly, it wants to know why! There is no obscure fact, no exotic street food, no distant travel destination too far out of reach for Curiosity to seek, try or explore.

Curiosity cannot travel straight from point A to point B. It must dive into every side street, poke into every shop, and browse every shelf of the dusty bookstore. Curiosity wants to see the main attraction, sure, but also every other attraction and the things that attract no one else.

Curiosity may be a core value for you if you have an insatiable appetite for knowledge and new experiences. Some people (you might see them as sticks in the mud) find your endless questions annoying. Nobody seems to understand why you read random Wikipedia articles or dive into YouTube rabbit holes just for fun. And they certainly do not want to try a fried grasshopper — but you know they are just an excellent (if salty) source of protein!

Mantra:

My thirst for understanding is my superpower.

Question: (Oh, like I need to provide you with more questions!)

45
Focus

Focus is the value of unwavering attention. Focus knows what it wants and can concentrate with laser-like intensity on it, sometimes for hours on end. Its superpower is the ability to set all else aside in service of its highest priority.

Imagination and Vision will guide you to the "what" in your life. Love, Family, or Faith may guide you to the "why." Focus, like Courage or Fairness, can guide the "how." Focus is how dreams turn into plans, actions, and results.

Focus recognizes the difference between "nice to have" and "essential." It identifies what is critical and zeroes in until the work is complete. Focus sets priorities as effortlessly as others breathe the air.

If Focus is one of your core values, you are single-minded once you have defined a course of action. You move steadily toward your goals, pushing aside or ignoring the non-essential. You see obstacles and distractions for what they are, and overcome them with little difficulty for as long as you have your target in sight. People admire you for your ability to maintain your Focus even in chaotic circumstances. You may see people who don't share this core value as "flaky" or daydreamers. Remember that while Focus is a fantastic value for productivity, it can be limiting if it becomes too extreme. It's okay to let yourself take a day off from time to time!

Mantra:

I am focused on the things that matter most.

Question: What is the best way for me to evaluate my goals regularly, so I can always be confident I am focused on the right things?

46
Family

Family is the value of closeness with a core group of other people with whom you share absolute and unconditional love. Family holds "your people" as your highest priority, whether it's your spouse and children, your parents, your siblings, other blood relatives or the people who have become your "chosen family" through long years of close friendship.

Family takes care of its own. When you consider someone Family, they are "one of yours." Whatever they need that you can provide will be done, regardless of the time or place, cost or inconvenience. Family is there for the one who needs a ride home at 2 a.m. or needs a place to stay for the night, or the week. Family comforts the victim of a car break-in or a relationship break-up. Family celebrates little victories, consoles devastating failures, and puts up with annoying habits and irritating moods.

Family is often the target of grand pronouncements about "work-life balance," and for that reason can be both an antidote to workaholism and an excuse to take a little too much time off. Finding the balance is important here, as is holding business leaders accountable for honoring and enforcing policies that support that balance.

When Family is one of your core values, you treasure the

moments you spend in the company of your closest kin. You invest significant time and energy in nurturing healthy relationships, open communication and quality time with them. It goes without saying that you love your Family with all your heart, and better yet than that, you *like* them and enjoy being with them.

Mantra:

I hold my family close to my heart every day.

Question: How does my commitment to my family help each of its members become their best selves?

47
Wellness

Wellness is the value of self-care. Wellness values health and harmony of body, mind, and spirit. It prioritizes the self, not because it is selfish, but because it recognizes the wisdom that "I cannot give what I do not have." By ensuring its own health and fitness, Wellness optimizes its capacity to serve and care for others.

Wellness is comprehensive, going beyond physical heath to cultivate soundness of mind and fullness of heart. Wellness makes time and space for these activities, recognizing that holistic well-being is a process, not an event. In this pursuit, Wellness leads to a sense of being adequately suited and prepared to fulfill any role or purpose required.

When you prioritize Wellness as a core value, you know that time spent on healthy habits is time well spent. It is likely that you enjoy and prefer wholesome foods, choose to engage in a regular program of exercise, spend time in prayer or meditation or reflection, and enjoy being in nature. Your self-care rituals are an important part of your life, and you know they play a big role in energizing you to meet the challenges of your day.

> **Mantra:**
>
> Taking care of myself helps me
> care better for others.

Question: What boundaries do I need to create to be sure I have time and space for my self-care?

48
Authenticity

Authenticity is the value of "what you see is what you get." Authenticity is true to itself. It never seems to be other than what it is; it never wears masks. The ultimate goal of Authenticity is to become fully itself, by deeply understanding itself and growing every day to become more of what it is.

Authenticity is consistent. It sticks to its guns, speaking and behaving according to its values and principles no matter the situation. Authenticity speaks its heart's truth, even when that truth is a little awkward or uncomfortable. Authenticity is never afraid to be what it is and makes no apology.

Authenticity also recognizes the difference between consistency and stagnation. It understands that change happens — we grow, evolve, develop — and something that felt right and true a year ago might not feel right and true now. The continuous search to know the self lies at the heart of Authenticity.

If you hold Authenticity as a core value, people know you. Your choices or your actions do not surprise them, because they consistently reflect your values. Those who know you will seek your opinion because they know you will not lie or exaggerate, either in favor or against them. People are generally at ease with you because they know they can trust you. Those who are very insecure in themselves, or who have something to hide, may find your presence unnerving.

Mantra:

I am what I am!

Question: Is there any area of my life where I find it challenging to be my authentic self? If so, what do I need to do to change that situation?

49
Adventure

Adventure is the value of bold action. Similar to curiosity but braver, Adventure is always ready to try something a little crazy for the sheer thrill of it! Adventure is restless. It wants to get out and try new things and new ways of doing old things. It loves variety, novelty, anything unusual or exotic. Adventure can't wait for the next opportunity to experience something unique.

Adventure cannot tolerate the same old same old. It needs to get out of the house, break the routine, run into the unknown with joyful abandon. It is the value of cross-country backpacking trips and camping out in the backyard; of climbing Kilimanjaro; of trying street food in Singapore; or checking out the taco truck a couple of blocks away. It is energetic, playful, and indefatigable even after a 14-hour plane ride or a run-in with poison ivy.

If Adventure is a core value for you, you have traveled as far as your time and budget will permit, and you're planning your next trip. You dream of far-off places, both real and imaginary, and what it would be like to be there. The desires you describe — perfectly reasonable to you — may sound insane to those who cherish a predictable routine and a warm bed. Remember to be patient with them. They are good people. They just don't understand.

> **Mantra:**
>
> Second star to the right,
> and straight on 'til morning!

Question: When I can't be traveling the world on a grand adventure, how can I bring a sense of adventure into my daily life at home?

50
Connection

Connection is exactly what it sounds like: the value of connecting with other people. Connection loves to be paired, partnered, and part of a team. It seeks out points of commonality and loves to find and flock with its "birds of a feather." Connection is the social butterfly that helps people find like-minded or complementary people.

Connection is an empathetic value that sees each person's worth and appreciates getting to know them. Connection knows a guy who does that, whatever "that" may be. It especially loves to "make connections" either connecting directly to another or introducing people whose acquaintance can serve their mutual benefit.

Connection is also about particular people you know, and want to know better. It will seek out specific people to enrich its network or to serve as mentors. Connection doesn't fawn, or "collect," or name-drop, but builds a strong web of genuine relationships with people who can help each other.

If Connection is a core value for you, you are a natural networker. You love to "hook people up" to those who share their interests or who can help them tackle their challenges. Customer service and sales jobs may be a natural fit for you, because talking to people and helping them accomplish their goals is one of your favorite pastimes. If you haven't already, you owe it to your community to join your local Chamber of Commerce!

Mantra:

I am a one-person Butterfly Effect -
the world changes for the better
when I connect people together.

Question: Who are two people you know who haven't met, and need to? (Ask yourself this at least once a week!)

51
Kindness

Kindness is the value of gentle care. Kindness does good things for others with no thought of recognition or recompense. It also does good things for itself, recognizing (as Wellness does) that the ability to serve others is predicated on keeping the self well cared for. Kindness is especially moved to care for those who are hurting. It seeks to give comfort and sanctuary from suffering.

Kindness, while gentle, possesses a profound strength, going above and beyond the call of duty to support those it touches. Importantly, Kindness does not "reach down" or "reach back" but goes side-by-side or even from below or behind to lift others up. In so doing, Kindness creates an environment that ensures that people feel great about themselves, finding their agency and strength.

We tragically undervalue Kindness as a value when fierce competition, tribalism or divisiveness takes hold in a community or in an organization. When it finds the courage to express itself fully, Kindness can change hearts in a way that the most compelling "logical" argument never will.

If Kindness is a core value for you, people know you as a caregiver. Your words and actions help people feel valued, nurtured, and loved. You may excel in fields like health care or working with kids, but don't limit yourself to those environments — you are desperately needed everywhere. Be aware of your boundaries and limits, as you may be prone to taking care of everyone else at your expense.

Mantra:

My strength is in my gentleness.

Question: Where in my world does kindness seem to be missing? How can I help?

52
Inclusion

Inclusion is the value of embracing every person's unique contribution. Inclusion welcomes every person into the "big tent", encouraging each one to bring their best selves into the process. Inclusion loves to make new friends, especially when they are different, because Inclusion recognizes that diversity of thought leads to more ideas and better solutions.

Inclusion understands that representation matters — that people function best when they feel seen, heard, and appreciated. It therefore actively seeks out fresh perspectives, differing points of view, and people whose base of experience is not the same. Inclusion doesn't even mind a spirited argument, if the process is respectful and the result is an approach that hadn't been considered. Inclusion understands that the vision will be achieved only when everyone has a fair shot at building it together.

If Inclusion is a core value for you, you have either always known, or recently realized that every person has worth, dignity, and something valuable to bring to the table. You are anything but "blind" to differences — you see and appreciate people who don't look like you, don't think like you, and don't speak like you. You want to know their stories. You may have a professional or personal role as an advocate for people who have been denied opportunities because of some aspect of their identity. You are passionate about ensuring that everyone has a voice in the big conversations of life.

Mantra:

I make sure everyone has a seat at the table.

Question: When I encounter a person who does not value inclusion or tries to shut others out, how does my inclusion value help me reach them?

Epilogue

Now that you have spent some time reading, writing, reflecting and talking about these 52 values, I hope you have discovered four to six core values that resonate with you and inspire you to live them as best you can. Maybe you gained some clarity about your values? Maybe you realized that your true core values differ from what you thought? Maybe you found the right words to express something you knew all along?

In writing this book, I even revised my list of values.

If, in reading this book, you discover that your core values aren't what you thought they were (or you are just discovering what they are), you may notice that your past behaviors and choices were not reflective of your beliefs, or that your beliefs invite, or require, ways of behaving that you hadn't considered. You might realize that what you thought were your guideposts of behavior aren't working for you. It's worth your time to reflect on what is changing — or what was never true in the first place — and decide how you would like to live your life differently. It is also possible — even likely — that you have discovered something important. You've thought of one (or more) I didn't include?

I would love to hear from you about your experience with the book, and what you learned about yourself and your values. I'd also love to hear about the value (or values) you discovered that weren't in the book. Send me your definitions and stories, and let's talk about them.

You can reach me at alan@elevationsunlimited.us.

Thanks for choosing to spend some time with this book, and if in the process you have realized you could use some additional help or a sounding board for your development, reach out to me.

Alan

About the Author

Alan Kovitz was born in Brooklyn, New York and spent his early childhood there and in Queens, New York. His family moved to New Jersey, where he graduated from Hightstown High School.

After a short stint at Rutgers University, Alan graduated from Tarkio College with a Bachelor's Degree in Business Administration and Economics. He immediately studied at the Joseph Katz Business School at the University of Pittsburgh, earning his MBA with a concentration in Human Resources.

Alan has worked in many fields since, concentrating on Sales and General Management. With his brother Adam, Alan started Elevations Unlimited in 2000, working with organizations in Strategic Planning, Sales Development and Leadership Development. He now concentrates on coaching entrepreneurs and those with entrepreneurial minds.

Alan lives with his partner Angela Lewis in Dover, Delaware. They enjoy their five children and eight grandchildren. In his spare time, Alan thrives on travel and following his favorite sports teams.

Acknowledgements

Thanks to Carolyn Flower and her amazing team at Oxygen Publishing for helping me see this project to its end. The expertise shared has created an excellent platform for this book's success.

With his editing help and cheerful banter, my editor, Richard Tardif, made the tedious chore easier to handle.

Thanks also to Laura Willis and Wendy Newell, who both read the manuscript later in the game and speak glowingly about its power to all - I am grateful.

CPSIA information can be obtained
at www.ICGtesting.com
Printed in the USA
LVHW010704211221
706820LV00007B/99